MANHATTAN

IN PHOTOGRAPHS

MANHATTAN

IN PHOTOGRAPHS

In collaboration with the travel experts at Fodor's

Marcia Reiss

GRAMERCY BOOKS
NEW YORK

© 2005 PRC Publishing Limited,
The Chrysalis Building,
Bramley Road, London W10 6SP

An imprint of **Chrysalis** Books Group plc

This 2005 edition is published by Gramercy Books, an imprint of Random House Value Publishing, a division of Random House, Inc., New York, by arrangement with Chrysalis Books, London.

Gramercy is a registered trademark and the colophon is a trademark of Random House, Inc.

Random House
New York • Toronto • London • Sydney • Auckland
www.randomhouse.com

Printed and bound in China

A catalog record for this title is available from the Library of Congress.

ISBN 0-517-22656-1

10 9 8 7 6 5 4 3 2 1

Credits
Editor: Anne McDowall
Designer: John Heritage
Picture Researcher: Rebecca Sodergren
Production: Alice Reeves
Reproduction: Anorax Imaging Ltd

Additional captions
Page 1: Old Merchant's House Museum, Greenwich Village
Page 2: Aerial view of Central Park

Contents

INTRODUCTION

New York may be the most photographed city in the world. Its icons—the Empire State Building, Times Square, United Nations, Chrysler Building, and many other famous sites—are instantly recognizable to people across the globe. All of these places can be found on one slender island, just 13 miles long by two miles wide.

The island of Manhattan—the smallest in area yet most intensely developed of the five boroughs of New York City—is the place all New Yorkers call "the city." Known for its canyons of skyscrapers, it also has wonderful parks and enough open sky and water around the island to give millions of residents and visitors welcome breathing room and astonishing

views. The scenes that are captured in this book provide a virtual tour of a dramatically diverse and exciting metropolis.

Manhattan in Photographs begins where the city began, in Lower Manhattan at the southern tip of the island. It follows the city's geography, covering each major neighborhood from south to north—or as New Yorkers say, from downtown to uptown. Each area is filled with many different views of famous buildings, parks, street scenes, restaurants, theaters, and other New York attractions. The photographs provide a comprehensive picture of the city today, while captions and neighborhood introductions present capsules of its fascinating history.

Manhattan's vitality is constantly renewed by its ever-changing nature. Over the course of its historic settlement, this long finger of land has pointed the way to new developments, molding and reshaping neighborhoods along its entire length. Just a year after the end of the Civil War, in the midst of a furious pace of new construction, the Manhattan diarist

▼ **East River View:** *Surrounded by rivers, New York is a city of dramatic contrasts—towering buildings against a backdrop of striking scenery. Sixteen miles long and spanned by six bridges, the East River is not a river at all, but a powerful tidal strait between the Atlantic Ocean and Long Island Sound. The Brooklyn and Manhattan bridges are shown in this view.*

George Templeton Strong noted that "a new town has been built on top of the old one and another excavated under it." His observation has been true ever since. Constantly rebuilding and reinventing itself, Manhattan has been a perpetual-motion machine of innovation and change.

Even some of Manhattan's most famous landmarks have moved from place to place. The Broadway Theater District did not start out on Broadway in Times Square. Originally on the Bowery in Lower Manhattan, it moved to Union Square and finally to Times Square in the 1890s. Tiffany's, a fixture on Fifth Avenue and the most famous jewelry store in the country, came to Manhattan's elegant shopping district from a series of different downtown locations. Even the Statue of Liberty moved around —that is, part of it did. Her colossal hand and torch were on display for nearly ten years in Madison Square Park while funds were raised to assemble the whole statue in New York Harbor in 1886.

Like the profile of a medieval city, the New York skyline was no higher than its church spires from colonial times through the first half of the nineteenth century. The tower on tiny St. Paul's Chapel, erected in 1796 in Lower Manhattan, made it the city's tallest building until Trinity Church rose higher in 1846. Troops of commercial buildings marched up the skyline in the second half of the century, yet the tallest structure built in this period was not a building at all, but the Brooklyn Bridge—the world's greatest construction project of the century. As the bridge towers rose in the 1870s, they surpassed the height and scale of every building in the city.

New York rose to power, not as a center of religion or government, but on a foundation of commerce. Recognizing the city's strategic location as a port, government and business leaders ringed Manhattan with new docks and rail lines after the Civil War. By the start of the twentieth century, monumental buildings such as the U.S. Custom House and Grand Central Terminal proclaimed New York's leading roles in trade and commerce.

▲ **Trinity Church and Graveyard:** *Nestled in a skyscraper canyon, this famous church was once the tallest on the New York skyline and it still asserts its dignity in the midst of the Financial District. Its churchyard, established in 1681, is a green retreat in this urban setting. The gravesites include many famous names from American history, notably Alexander Hamilton and Robert Fulton.*

▶ **New York Taxi:** *As familiar as the Statue of Liberty, yellow taxis are an unmistakable part of New York City's iconography. A popular form of transportation since the early 1900s, taxis were not always yellow: it wasn't until 1967 that all licensed cabs were required to wear the color. This is a view of Park Avenue, which becomes a yellow streak of taxis during rush hour.*

While unbridled economic forces led to raging development, civic leaders and private citizens at times placed a temperate hand on the city's growth. Central Park, the largest public works project of the nineteenth century (1856–78), preserved more than 800 acres of undeveloped land for public use—a major chunk of the city's size at that time. Grand buildings, such as the Metropolitan Museum of Art (1874–1926), American Museum of Natural History (1877–1924), and the New York Public Library (1911) also committed vast resources to the public good. Greenwich Village residents—nonconformists at heart—often protested large-scale developments and preserved much of their neighborhood's historic village atmosphere.

At first, the city looked to Europe for its architectural style and authenticity. But Manhattan soon made its own unmistakable mark. Forged by steel construction and high-speed elevators in the late nineteenth century, the skyscraper revolutionized architecture and gave Manhattan a new symbol for its financial power. After the turn of the century, its skyline began to look like that of no other city in the world. Like the glaciers that shaped the island's rocky escarpment, skyscrapers spread from one end of Manhattan to the other, carving out new mountain ranges of buildings.

The Flatiron Building rose in 1903 like the prow of a ship, leading development into new waters beyond Lower Manhattan. Commercial buildings became as important as churches and imitated their styles. The Neo-Gothic detail on the Woolworth Building (1913) made it a "Cathedral of Commerce." In turn, churches imitated commercial buildings. At 24 stories high, Riverside Church in Harlem (1930) was a skyscraper church.

As new buildings shaped the city, the face of its population also changed. By 1898—the year Manhattan joined with the other four boroughs to form Greater New York City—half of its population was foreign born. Arriving first from Europe and later from every part of the globe, polyglot New Yorkers have infused the city with cultural diversity and created its extraordinary cosmopolitanism.

Great buildings and parks extended Manhattan's frontiers. Construction of Central Park pushed the city northward, leading to the development of two

major neighborhoods flanking the park, the Upper East and Upper West Sides. In the first decade of the twentieth century, Grand Central Terminal built a city within a city on top of its railroad tracks. The immense project created stylish Park Avenue and turned New York's northern outskirts into Midtown, a new office district that rivaled Wall Street as the skyscraper kingdom. In the 1920s, the Chrysler Building, a vision of fantasy, was one of dozens of towers racing to become the tallest in the world. In 1931, the Empire State Building became king of the sky, just before the Depression brought the race to a screeching halt.

In the lean years of the Depression, Rockefeller Center (1932–40) emerged as the city's largest private real-estate venture and a sophisticated model of urban planning. The building boom that followed World War II brought masterpieces of modern, innovative design. The United Nations Secretariat building (1953) was the city's first glass tower. Frank Lloyd Wright's spiraling Guggenheim Museum (1959) broke away from traditional design on elegant Fifth Avenue. The Lever House (1952) and Seagram Building (1958) changed Park Avenue from a line of masonry buildings to a glass showcase of corporate towers. The towers kept rising throughout the 1960s and 1970s, reaching new heights with the 110-story twin towers of the World Trade Center in 1972.

To many New Yorkers and visitors alike, Manhattan will never be the same without the twin towers. But as new plans for Ground Zero move forward, the city can take heart in remembering the transformation of many of its neighborhoods that had fallen on hard times.

Drug dealers, pornography, and prostitution dominated Times Square from the 1960s through the 1980s. Even the heart of the Broadway Theater District, West 42nd Street, had become a notoriously squalid strip. After years of efforts by government and private groups, Times Square has finally overcome its sleazy reputation. Reborn in the 1990s as

▶ **Greenwich Village Brownstone:** *In a city of towering proportions, Greenwich Village brings Manhattan back to a human scale. While other parts of the city have changed dramatically over time, historic Village homes retain a graceful, timeless quality.*

the "New 42nd Street," the block shines brighter than ever before with elegantly refurbished theaters and glittering new attractions.

In the 1970s, Central Park also had a bad name. Vandalism and crime stalked its pastoral landscape: tourists avoided the park completely, while New Yorkers used it with caution. In 1980, however, a nonprofit group, the Central Park Conservancy, began to raise private funds to restore and maintain the park. To date, the group has raised more than $300 million and Central Park has become a city showpiece once again.

Once lined with slender piers, graceful ships, and every kind of cargo, Manhattan's Hudson River waterfront literally lost its edge when the major shipping lines began to move to New Jersey's immense container ports in the 1950s. The old pier sheds crumbled into the river leaving a toothless stretch of waterfront with a few stubby survivors here and

▼ **Chinatown:** *Manhattan is filled with ethnic neighborhoods, but Chinatown is one of the largest and most colorful. Once the most populous Chinese community in the western hemisphere, the Manhattan enclave has spread throughout the city's five boroughs.*

there. Today, the riverfront is getting its smile back as the five-mile-long Hudson River Park takes shape with new recreation piers and tree-lined esplanade.

Abandoned factories and marginal office buildings in many areas have also come back to life. In neighborhoods such as SoHo and TriBeCa, they have been converted to apartments, shops, and restaurants. Even after the terror and heartbreak of September 11, New Yorkers have been returning, not only to work, but also to live in Lower Manhattan, all around the twin towers site. New Yorkers have come back to Manhattan for the same reasons they have always chosen to live here—to experience the city's inextinguishable vitality. While other cities have expanded at their edges through suburban sprawl, Manhattan has concentrated its growth within its island borders, distilling the essence of the metropolis in an irresistible urban brew.

▼ **Central Park Lake:** *Against the spectacular backdrop of the city, the lake in Central Park is one of the most scenic features of New York today. This view looks toward apartment towers on the Upper West Side, one of the neighborhoods that grew up around the park after it was completed in the 1870s.*

East Midtown Waterfront: *The evolution of New York skyscrapers unfolds in this sweeping view. The U.N. Secretariat building (1953), left, was the city's first glass-walled tower. The tip of the Empire State Building spire can be seen rising above the right-hand corner of the Secretariat. Later advances in technology allowed the three towers to the right, the U.N. Plaza Buildings (1976–83), to be tautly wrapped in glass. To the far right is the Chrysler Building (1930), from an earlier age of brick-and-steel construction.*

Lower Manhattan

Shaped like Manhattan's big toe, this one-and-a-half-mile triangle south of Canal Street is where Dutch settlers established a foothold in the New World in 1624. It is where the city began, and where, over the centuries, it became a mix of everything that made New York famous. This is the home of the powerful financial center of Wall Street, the historic Port of New York, the ethnic melting pot of the Lower East Side, the towering skyline at the tip of the island, and the tragic void of Ground Zero, the former site of the World Trade Center.

As new plans for the World Trade Center site develop, the old areas of Lower Manhattan are also being recharged. TriBeCa and SoHo, two industrial areas with distinctive cast-iron warehouses, now feature some of the most expensive loft apartments and trendiest shops in the city. The Lower East Side, America's gateway to millions of immigrants a century ago, is still the place for flavorful food and bargain shopping. While its ethnic history is evident even today, many of its old tenements have been converted to upscale apartments and are filling up with young professionals. Chinatown, once a slice of the Lower East Side, has taken over most of the pie, crossing over into Little Italy and serving Peking duck next to the area's pizza parlors.

Battery Park City and the World Financial Center—a long line of residential and office towers nearly as big as a city itself—were built along the Hudson River in the 1980s and are still growing. Historic Battery Park at the tip of the island is having a total makeover. This is the place where many visitors begin their tour of Manhattan, taking a boat ride to the Statue of Liberty and Ellis Island.

▶ **Statue of Liberty:** *Recognized throughout the world, this icon of America needs no description. But her colossal measurements should not be missed up close. The statue's iron skeleton was engineered by Gustave Eiffel, the very one who built the Eiffel Tower. From the tip of her flaming torch to the base of her pedestal, the statue rises 395 feet above the harbor, while her index finger alone is eight feet long. Boats to the statue leave from Battery Park and also dock at Ellis Island.*

◀ **Lower Manhattan Waterfront:** *Towers rise at the southern tip of the island, called the Battery, after a row of guns that marked the shoreline in colonial times. Peter Stuyvesant, the Dutch governor of New Amsterdam, stood here in 1664 and stomped his wooden leg as the British sailed in to take over the colony. Today, you can walk on what was water in Stuyvesant's time. The sea wall, extended by landfill over the centuries, has a restored walkway that affords panoramic harbor views.*

▶ **Castle Clinton National Monument:** *Built to deter the British from attacking New York in the War of 1812, this castle, actually a fort, did the job with nary a shot fired. Later, it became Castle Garden, a popular music hall, then an aquarium. Nearly demolished in the 1940s, it was saved by a public campaign and preserved as a national monument. Today, it is also a museum and the place to buy tickets to the Statue of Liberty and Ellis Island.*

▶ **Battery Park Memorial:** *A powerful sculpture of an eagle is the centerpiece of a memorial to more than 4500 servicemen who died off the East Coast in World War II. Their names are engraved on eight granite slabs surrounding the sculpture in Battery Park.*

◀ **Ellis Island/National Museum of Immigration:** *Standing on wind-swept Ellis Island and looking across the waters to Lower Manhattan, one can imagine how millions of immigrants, arriving here after long, arduous voyages, still felt a bit at sea. Sixteen million passed through the island's great entry hall from 1892 to 1929. After decades of deterioration, the French Renaissance-style building has now been beautifully restored as a National Museum of Immigration.*

Staten Island Ferry:

One of the city's best bargains, the ferry ride between Lower Manhattan and Staten Island offers spectacular views—all for free. In operation since 1905, the double-decker boats carry thousands of commuters each day and are as familiar in the harbor as taxis on the streets. Whether or not you plan to visit Staten Island, the ferry crossing itself, which takes about 25 minutes each way, is well worth the trip.

Governors Island:

Minutes away from Lower Manhattan, this small island at the entrance to the harbor is a former military base with an elegant Georgian-style village. Off-limits for centuries, it was opened to public tours in 2003. Ferries leave, mid-June through Labor Day, from the Battery Maritime Building next to Battery Park.

▲ **Fraunces Tavern:**
This handsome building is a
recreation of the tavern
where George Washington
delivered the famous farewell
to his officers at the end of
the American Revolution in
1783. It is part of a block of
historic buildings, the few
remaining eighteenth-century
structures amid the towers of
Lower Manhattan. The tavern
includes a museum of historic
exhibits and a restaurant
that is decorated in period
furnishings.

▶ **Federal Hall**
National Memorial: This is
the spot—although not the
actual building—where
George Washington took the
oath of office as first U.S.
president. It is also the site
where the American Stamp
Act Congress made its
protest against the British
for "taxation without
representation." This building,
erected in 1842, is a
magnificent example of the
Greek Revival style.

◀ **Wall Street Bull:** *This sculpture made a surprise appearance on Wall Street when its creator delivered it on a flatbed truck one early morning in 1989. Italian sculptor Arturo Di Modica donated it to the city as a sign of American resurgence after the stock market crash of 1987. Since then this embodiment of a raging bull market has become a symbol of capitalism itself. Tourists love to grab it by the horns.*

▶ **New York Stock Exchange Building:** *Behind the building's stately classical façade, the great trading floor pulses with excitement. It all began on this Wall Street corner in 1792 with 22 stockbrokers meeting under a tree. The present building, completed in 1903, is crowned by a pediment containing an allegorical sculpture. Its title, "Integrity Protecting the Rights of Man," could be a warning to today's financial dealers.*

◀ **U.S. Customs House:** *In the days before income tax, the U.S. government collected its greatest revenues from customs duties. As the nation's center of trade, New York City pulled in the lion's share at this grand, turn-of-the-century building. Today, its splendid interior is home to the National Museum of the American Indian, a branch of the Smithsonian collection.*

◀ **Trinity Church:** *New York's leading families of the nineteenth century worshipped within this Neo-Gothic sanctuary in Lower Manhattan and added to its splendor. The stained-glass window towering above the altar depicts religious figures in a dazzling array of colors.*

▲ **South Street Seaport Pier:** *This part of Lower Manhattan was the heart of the Port of New York in the nineteenth and early twentieth centuries. Filled with the sounds and smells of the sea, it was packed with ships, horses, wagons, and people of every trade, all jostling for space. Today, a fleet of historic ships preserves a sense of the past within the modern city. You can climb aboard them and even take an excursion.*

Winter Garden: *One of the few places with palm trees in New York City, this vaulted glass building is a magical space. Across the street from the World Trade Center towers, it miraculously survived the attacks of September 11, 2001, and has reopened with restaurants and shops on several levels, plus a full schedule of concerts and special events.*

Museum of Jewish Heritage: *Opened in 2002, the pyramid-top museum is a striking architectural addition to the many attractions on the Battery Park City Esplanade, a mile-long walkway along the Hudson River. Exhibits include a timeline of Jewish history and a memorial to the victims of the Holocaust. Personal objects, photographs, and original films illustrate the story of Jewish heritage in the twentieth century.*

▷ **St. Paul's Chapel:**

Dwarfed by modern skyscrapers today, St. Paul's steeple was Manhattan's tallest tower from 1796 to 1846. The chapel is Manhattan's oldest public building in continuous use.

▲ **St. Paul's Chapel:**
The space behind St. Paul's
steeple, illuminated by the
Tribute of Light, was once
filled by the World Trade
Center towers. Remarkably
spared when the towers
collapsed, the chapel served
as a respite center for
thousands of volunteers who
pored through the mountains
of debris searching for the
victims' remains.

▶ **World Trade Center
Tribute of Light:** *Six
months after the attacks of
September 11, 2001, shafts
of light rose from the spot
where the World Trade
Center towers once stood.
The display, seen throughout
the city, was a moving tribute
to the thousands who died,
and a symbol of renewal for
the city. A new Freedom
Tower, memorial plaza, and
performing arts center are
planned for the site.*

◀ **City Hall:** *It may seem like an incongruous place for New York City's rough-and-tumble politics, but this French Renaissance mini-palace is still the seat of government. The mayor and City Council conduct daily business here as they have done for the past two centuries. Although the building is not open to the public, it is well worth the trip to see the historic exterior and take a stroll through lovely City Hall Park.*

▶ **City Hall Interior:** *City Hall's striking interior is a hidden gem, accessible only to those on official business. This striking pair of staircases, curving up to a magnificent dome, awaits those fortunate enough to be allowed inside the front door.*

◀ **Tweed Courthouse:**

History has paid an ironic tribute to the infamous Boss Tweed, who embezzled millions of dollars by inflating the construction costs of this elaborate courthouse in the 1870s. Tried and convicted in this very building, he went to jail, but the courthouse, forever after known by his name, went on to become one of the greatest achievements in the city's panoply of civic architecture. This is a view of the rotunda, the center of 30 ornate courtrooms. The building currently houses the Department of Education.

▲ **Woolworth Building:**

The tallest building in the world for the first 17 years of its life, the Woolworth Building reigned over the New York skyline until it lost its title to the Chrysler Building in 1930. It was built for the dime-store king, Frank Woolworth, in 1913, but even though his national empire of stores has disappeared, the Woolworth Building has remained an architectural legend.

▲ **Federal Courthouse:**
This monumental courthouse
has been the setting for law-
and-order dramas, both real
and imagined. With cameras
flashing, notorious criminals,
terrorists, and, even, Martha
Stewart have walked up
these stairs to face trial. The
building was also featured in a
memorable scene from the
first Godfather film, in which
Mafia chieftains were gunned
down on the steep flight of
steps.

▶ **Brooklyn Bridge:** The
bridge towers were New
York's first skyscrapers, rising
higher and plunging deeper
into bedrock than any other
building had done before. Its
span was longer than that of
any other bridge in the world.
Today, it is the beauty of the
Brooklyn Bridge that captures
the imagination. A walk over
it is one of the great New
York experiences.

◀ **Chinatown Store
Window:** *The color and
flavor of Chinatown is evident
throughout the many shops
and restaurants of this
bustling district. Plied with
Asian foods and herbs of
every kind, its grocery stores
attract not only local
residents, but also savvy
cooks throughout the city.*

▲ **Chinatown Street
Signs:** *These hand-lettered
signs on a Chinatown street
leave no doubt that the
neighborhood is still
authentically Chinese.
Beginning in the early
nineteenth century, the
enclave spread from a few
blocks to a large and distinct
section of the Lower East
Side. By 1980, New York
City's Chinese community had
become the largest in the
country, surpassing the one in
San Francisco.*

◄ **Buddhist Temple:** *A Buddhist temple provides a quiet retreat off Chinatown's crowded streets. Many other local buildings—banks, schools, and other centers of everyday life—are also decorated in red lacquer and embellished with Pagoda-style details.*

▶ **Manhattan Bridge:** *This steel suspension bridge over the East River has a monumental entrance—a horseshoe-shaped colonnade at Canal Street in Chinatown. You can walk or bike to Brooklyn on the pedestrian walkway on the upper level, or take the subway train over the river on the lower level.*

▶ **Little Italy Festival:** *Little Italy was in its heyday in the 1880s after waves of Italian immigrants washed over the northern part of Lower Manhattan. By the 1960s, the younger generation had moved to suburbia, leaving most of the neighborhood to expanding numbers of Chinese arrivals. But Mulberry Street still retains its Italian flavor, especially during the Feast of San Gennaro each September.*

Lower East Side Tenement Museum: *The first actual tenement to be preserved as a museum, this humble dwelling is a monument to the struggling families who made their way through New York City during its peak years of immigration. More than ten thousand people lived in this single building between 1870 and 1915, though not all at once. Visitors can enter several carefully restored apartments to experience something of the lives of a few of the actual residents from different countries and historical periods.*

Puck Building: *The humor magazine Puck was produced in this building from 1887 to 1918. Its namesake, and the magazine's logo, was the Shakespearean character who famously proclaimed, "What fools these mortals be". Puck's gilt statue is perched on a corner ledge, watching over students who attend New York University's Graduate School of Public Service, which is now located in the building.*

Greenwich Village

This neighborhood of tree-lined streets and historic rowhouses has always been a welcome place for different lifestyles. Artists, musicians, and free spirits of all kinds mingle happily with those of more genteel tastes. In Washington Square Park, the center of the Village, soapbox oratory can often be heard against a background of impromptu folk, rock, and rap music. The lively activity is offset by the row of stately townhouses on the north side of the park, including several immortalized by Henry James in his novel *Washington Square*.

Gay and lesbian enclaves have long been ensconced on the narrow streets of the West Village, the heart of the gay-rights movement. Purple-haired, pierced denizens of the East Village also assert their individuality. The entire Village is an urban campus, laced with students from several local colleges. New York University, which is now spread throughout Greenwich Village, has been on Washington Square since 1837. Its faculty has included both Walt Whitman, who conducted poetry classes, and Thomas Wolfe, who taught fiction writing.

From the very beginning, Village residents were protective of their unique neighborhood. In the early 1800s, they convinced the Common Council, the governing body of the time, to exempt their crooked colonial lanes from the new rigid street grid imposed on the rest of the city. As a result, many Village streets are at odd angles to each other, winding along their own way. This independent spirit continued through the twentieth century as local groups fought to preserve many of the area's architectural treasures.

▶ **Greenwich Village Street:** *Tree-lined streets and nineteenth-century rowhouses typify many parts of Greenwich Village. In a city known for skyscrapers and concrete, this neighborhood has cast its charm on New Yorkers for centuries, preserving a village atmosphere within the metropolis.*

◀ **Washington Square Arch:** *The arch is the quintessential landmark of Greenwich Village, so much so that few people associate it with its original purpose, to commemorate the centenary of George Washington's inauguration. When it was built, originally of wood, in 1889, it was so beloved by New Yorkers that they contributed the funds to erect the permanent marble monument. The building framed by the arch is One Fifth Avenue, one of the first apartment towers built in this largely low-rise neighborhood.*

▲ **Judson Memorial Church:** *Like Greenwich Village itself, this architecturally eclectic church has hosted many lifestyles. Built in the 1890s, it was named after the first American Baptist missionary. During the beatnik and hippie eras of the 1950s and 1960s, it was a center for unusual theatrical and musical events, known as "happenings." Today, the bell tower is a dormitory for New York University students.*

◀ **Public Theater:** *Built in the 1850s as the city's first major library open to the public, this Italian Renaissance palazzo was saved from demolition in the 1960s by impresario Joseph Papp. He and a group of citizens persuaded city officials to purchase the building as a home for Papp's New York Shakespeare Festival. The elaborate interior was converted into three theaters, which have maintained a tradition for innovative productions.*

▲ **Blue Note Jazz Club:** *Although it has been open only since the 1980s, the Blue Note has earned its reputation as a world-class jazz joint. Legendary artists such as Ray Charles, Dizzy Gillespie, Oscar Peterson, Natalie Cole, and Tony Bennett have performed at this Greenwich Village hot spot, which also features big names in Blues, Latin, Brazilian, Fusion, R & B, and Soul music.*

Grace Church: *Years before he created the better-known St. Patrick's Cathedral, James Renwick designed this graceful Gothic Revival church in 1846. Located on a bend in Broadway, the small church stands out as a Greenwich Village landmark and is widely acclaimed as one of the city's architectural treasures.*

White Horse Tavern:
The tavern is well known for its famous patron, Dylan Thomas, and has a room dedicated to the Welsh poet's memory. One of the few wood-framed buildings left in Manhattan, this simple watering hole in the West Village dates to 1880. It survived as a speakeasy during Prohibition, became a popular meeting place for young writers and artists in the 1940s and 1950s, and is still a friendly hangout.

Old Merchant's House Museum: *The "old merchant" was Seabury Tredwell, who purchased this East Village house in 1835, just three years after it was built. Tredwells lived here for nearly a century until the last one died in 1933. A distant relative preserved the house and its furnishings. Now a public museum, it is perhaps the city's only Greek Revival house authentically intact inside and out.*

◄ **Jefferson Market Library:** *Greenwich Village residents mounted one of the earliest historic-preservation campaigns to save this prominent High-Victorian landmark. It was built as a courthouse in the 1870s, complete with a relief of the trial from the Merchant of Venice on its façade. Vacant and in precarious condition in the 1950s, it found new life in the 1960s, when it was restored as a library.*

▶ **McSorley's Old Ale House:** *Old photographs on tin-sheet walls and sawdust on the floor reinforce McSorley's claim to be the oldest saloon still operating in the city, since 1854. Before the 1970s, it served only men, but women are now welcome to join the old boy's atmosphere in this East Village setting.*

◄ **Hudson River Park:** *After decades of deterioration, Manhattan's Hudson River waterfront is being transformed into a five-mile-long linear park. The Greenwich Village section was the first to sprout trees, flowerbeds, and new recreation piers. The new piers were built over the decrepit remains of old docks, marking the historic locations and minimizing the impact on the river ecology.*

Union Square to Midtown

Known more to New Yorkers than tourists, this slice of Manhattan between Greenwich Village and Midtown includes a collection of intriguing neighborhoods: Union Square, Gramercy Park, Madison Square, the Flatiron District, and Chelsea. Historically and architecturally diverse, they have become some of the most interesting and desirable places to live and visit in Manhattan today.

Union Square, a park just north of Greenwich Village, was the site of workers' rallies and mass political protests from the Civil War well into the twentieth century. The park was refurbished in the 1980s and its popular farmer's market has led to a boom in gourmet restaurants on the surrounding blocks. A few blocks to the north, Gramercy Park, an exclusive neighborhood where former President Theodore Roosevelt was born, has retained its nineteenth-century charm. A bit further north is Madison Square, another urbane residential district laid out before the Civil War. Novelist Edith Wharton was born in this area. Her fashionable family, the Joneses, were the inspiration for the saying, "keeping up with the Joneses." The neighborhood was later transformed into a commercial district.

The landmark Flatiron Building stands across the street from Madison Square Park at Fifth Avenue and 23rd Street. In the early twentieth century, this windy intersection was part of the Ladies' Mile, a fashionable shopping district. Legend has it that a popular phrase of the day, "Twenty-three skidoo," was coined by policemen shooing away men who gawked at the windblown women on 23rd Street. To the west is Chelsea, a mix of industrial and residential buildings with a fascinating "Who's Who" of artists once in residence, from Mark Twain to Andy Warhol. Today, Chelsea is the city's newest art-gallery district.

▶ **Flatiron Building:** *Often mistaken for New York's first skyscraper, the Flatiron Building, completed in 1903, was not the first tower built on a steel frame. But its shape and location were so dramatic that it became a skyscraper icon and an unmistakable symbol of the city throughout the twentieth century. Rising on a triangular island between Fifth Avenue and Broadway, it literally stands out on its own.*

◄ **Gramercy Park:** *Laid out in 1831 as a gracious urban square, Gramercy Park remains one of the most charming residential districts in the city. Although only residents on the square have keys to the fenced park, it enhances the beauty of the entire area. Many original townhouses still surround the park, preserving an air of nineteenth-century elegance. The nearby birthplace of famous resident Theodore Roosevelt is a reconstruction of the past president's boyhood home.*

▶ **Metropolitan Life Insurance Tower:** *Modeled on the campanile of St. Mark's Square in Venice, this tower became the world's tallest in 1909. But even after it relinquished its title, it retained a special place in the night sky. Illuminated by floodlights, it became a symbol of the life insurance company's motto, "the Light that Never Fails."*

◀ **Pierpont Morgan Library:** *Magnificent yet intimate, this Italian Renaissance palazzo was built a century ago on fashionable Madison Avenue as the private library of financier Pierpont Morgan, an avid collector of rare manuscripts, drawings, and prints. After his death, his son, J.P. Morgan, Jr., fulfilled his father's wish of opening the library to the public. In 1991 it incorporated J.P.'s neighboring townhouse.*

▲ **Madison Square Park:** *The park got its name from the first two Madison Square Gardens—lavish predecessors to the modern sports arena in West Midtown. Beautifully restored in 2000, the park is an urban oasis pleasantly dotted with historic statuary, a fountain, benches, and a playground. Surrounded by many restaurants, it is a popular place at lunchtime.*

Chelsea Hotel: *The roster of residents at the Chelsea Hotel is a timeline of artistic changes. Mark Twain, O. Henry, Thomas Wolfe, Dylan Thomas, Arthur Miller, Sarah Bernhardt, Jackson Pollock, and guitarist Sid Vicious of the punk rock group "Sex Pistols" all called the Chelsea home. The building was the city's first co-operative apartment house and has been operating as a residence hotel since 1905.*

▲ **Chelsea Piers:** *Built in 1910 for legendary luxury liners like the Titanic, the Mauritania, and Lusitania, these piers were abandoned in the 1960s after their main tenant, United States Lines, moved to New Jersey. Now they house a sports complex, with Olympic-sized ice-skating rinks, a multi-level golf-driving range, and a number of facilities for children.*

▶ **Empire Diner:** *Even to first-time visitors, this round-the-clock diner in Chelsea often looks familiar. A piece of 1950s Americana, it is also a popular movie set for many films shot in New York City. Men in Black is just one recent example.*

West Midtown

Midtown is Manhattan's central business district and transportation hub—the part of the city most visitors know best. It covers the island's midriff, from 34th to 59th Streets, with Fifth Avenue as a shiny belt buckle dividing the East and West sections. Each section is chock full of major attractions. West Midtown, from the west side of Fifth to the Hudson River, has a list of famous places that reads like a city guide itself: the Empire State Building, Rockefeller Center, Radio City Music Hall, Macy's Department Store, Madison Square Garden, and the newly expanded Museum of Modern Art. Although Times Square also falls within West Midtown borders, it is a distinct neighborhood all by its glittering self.

While West Midtown offers a wealth of opportunities to see the sights, not all of them are indoors. In the midst of this bustling commercial district, you can picnic on the lush lawn of Bryant Park, which adjoins the New York Public Library on 42nd Street. Or sit on the library steps alongside a pair of friendly stone lions and watch the world go by on Fifth Avenue. Even the Museum of Modern Art offers a breath of fresh air from its enchanting sculpture garden.

Further west, you might go back inside to take in a basketball game or rock concert at Madison Square Garden, a 20,000-seat arena. Once you reach the river, you can stand on the deck of a World War II aircraft carrier, now the Intrepid Museum at West 46th Street, or board a Circle Line excursion boat at West 42nd Street for an exhilarating trip all around Manhattan Island.

▶ **Empire State Building:** *Reaching 102 stories in 1931, the Empire State Building was the tallest in the world for nearly half a century, until the completion of the 110-story World Trade Center towers in the 1970s. Since the collapse of the twin towers, the Empire State has dominated the New York skyline once again, a solemn king of the sky. The view from the observation deck at the top is a breath-taking experience, by day or night.*

◁ **Macy's Department Store:** *Macy's has dominated Herald Square since 1902, the year it moved up from its 14th Street location to become "the world's largest store." The square was a racy dance-hall district at the turn of the century, but once Macy's arrived, 34th Street and Broadway became the city's best-known shopping district.*

▲ **Midtown Pretzel Vendor:** *Street food is a must for busy New Yorkers and these big pretzels are a ubiquitous snack. Sold by pushcart vendors on nearly every midtown corner, the hot, salty treat is a favorite with people always on the go.*

New York Public Library: *Two city blocks in length, the Main Reading Room of the New York Public Library is a magnificent sanctuary in a classical temple of books. Located at Fifth Avenue and 42nd Street, the library replaced a massive water reservoir with walls 50 feet high that had occupied the site from 1842 to 1911. It is now the core research facility for an extensive citywide system of 85 neighborhood branches.*

Library Lions: *The pair of stone lions in front of the 42nd Street Library are among the best-known and most-loved statuary in the city. Regal, yet welcoming, they don wreaths in the Christmas Season and green hats on St. Patrick's Day and patiently pose for countless photos throughout the year.*

Bryant Park: *Once a dangerous drug hangout, this splendid midtown oasis was restored as a city showpiece in the 1990s. Below its lawn is a massive subterranean storage area for more than three million books from the adjacent New York Public Library. The park also rests on a historic site. New York's first World's Fair was held here in 1853 in the Crystal Palace— an enormous structure modeled after London's famous exhibition hall and destroyed only a few years later in a spectacular fire.*

▲ **Rockefeller Center:**
*Encompassing nearly 20
buildings, Rockefeller Center
was the largest private real-
estate venture ever
undertaken in New York City.
Criticized at first for its
enormous size, the center
was later seen as ahead of
its time and the premier
urban complex of the
twentieth century. The plaza,
with its gilded statue of
Prometheus, is a vibrant
center of activity.*

▶ **Radio City Music
Hall:** *The largest theater of
its time, Radio City Music hall
opened at the start of the
Depression and lost tens of
thousands of dollars in its
first weeks of operation.
Today, with its stunning Art
Deco interior completely
restored, it is one of the city's
most popular venues.*

◀ **Carnegie Hall:** *Steel magnate Andrew Carnegie built this concert hall as one of his many projects to "improve mankind." Famous for its wonderful acoustics, it has hosted the world's leading musicians, starting with the American conducting debut of Tchaikovsky in 1891. Nearly demolished in 1960, the Italian Renaissance-style building was purchased by the city and handsomely refurbished in later years.*

▶ **The Museum of Modern Art:** *Affectionately known as MoMA, this museum was the mother of contemporary art museums. It opened in 1939 and grew over the years along with the popularity of modern art, eventually outgrowing its collection. A major expansion, completed in 2004, carries on the style of the marble-and-glass original with much larger exhibition spaces and striking city views. The sculpture garden—a serene urban oasis—is one of the most popular features.*

◁ Jacob Javits Convention Center: *A modern version of London's Crystal Palace, this mammoth assemblage of glass and pre-fabricated steel boxes glows at night. Five blocks long and enclosing nearly two million square feet, it nonetheless is small by current convention-center standards. To compete with those in other cities, it is planning an expansion.*

▷ Madison Square Garden: *To sports and rock-concert fans, "the Garden," a huge arena built in 1968, is the ultimate venue. To those who remember the grand railroad station that it replaced, the modern building is a sorry reminder of the loss of a magnificent space. Although Penn Station still operates below, the railroad's vast waiting room and soaring iron-and-glass train sheds are only a memory. Their destruction sparked a preservation movement that has saved many other historic buildings in the city.*

▷ Intrepid Sea, Air and Space Museum: *This 900-foot-long aircraft carrier saw action in World War II and Vietnam. Now permanently docked on the Hudson River in West Midtown, it is the world's largest naval museum. More than 30 aircraft are displayed on the flight deck. Visitors can experience a virtual flight or climb inside a replica wooden submarine.*

Times Square

Although it got its name from the *New York Times* when the newspaper company moved to the intersection of Broadway and 42nd Street in 1904, Times Square has always had its own flashy personality. In the 1880s and 1890s, impresario Oscar Hammerstein I opened dazzling music halls and lavish theaters. By World War I, most of the city's legitimate theaters downtown had moved up to Times Square, creating the famous Broadway Theater District. In the 1920s, the marquees of more than 75 theaters on this "Great White Way" sparkled with the names of Broadway shows. Opulent movie palaces increased the glitter in the 1920s with the rise of the film industry. The first talking picture, *The Jazz Singer* with Al Jolson, had its debut on Broadway. Popular music composers and publishers made their headquarters in nearby Tin Pan Alley.

The peak of activity came crashing down with the stock market in 1929. During the years following the Depression, burlesque and peep shows, penny arcades, and dime-a-dance halls made the area the capitol of honky tonk. Although brothels had always existed on the fringes, by the late 1960s, prostitutes, drug trafficking, and pornographic movies had spread throughout the area. Dozens of legitimate theaters closed. The survivors retreated from Broadway to the side streets, but the sleaze followed—even to the Theater District's most famous address, West 42nd Street. After many failed clean-up efforts, the neighborhood finally was able to cast off its squalid past in the 1990s through a major investment of public and private funds. Restored theaters, new office towers, and family attractions have turned the bright lights on once again.

▶ **Times Square Tower:** *The familiar tower with the giant screen and flashing lights in the center of Times Square is a far cry from the first tower erected here a century ago. The original, a pink-granite Italian Renaissance-style building, housed the* New York Times *when it relocated from its old offices downtown. The paper moved in on New Year's Eve, 1904, and its spectacular fireworks display started a New York tradition, making it the place ever since for throngs of revelers to celebrate the New Year.*

◄ **Times Square Theater District:** *In the 1970s, pornographic movie houses swallowed up dozens of historic theaters, nearly killing legitimate theater on its home turf, West 42nd Street. Today, restorations like Disney's remake of the Art Nouveau New Amsterdam Theater have brought these architectural and cultural gems back to life.*

▶ **New 42nd Street Studios:** *Like the restored Theater District itself, this new building, a rehearsal studio for dance companies, is all lights and action. Computerized lasers wash over steel louvers on the façade, creating an ever-changing light show, a high-tech version of a Times Square marquee.*

▶ **Algonquin Hotel:** *Throughout the roaring 1920s, the Algonquin was the meeting place for the Round Table, a voluble gathering of the New York literati led by Vanity Fair drama critic Dorothy Parker. Recently refurbished, the hotel retains its historic clubby atmosphere.*

East Midtown

East Midtown is strung with stars of the New York skyline—the Chrysler Building, the United Nations, and the slant-roofed Citicorp Tower. Yet most of Midtown from Fifth Avenue to the East River lay undeveloped until the start of the twentieth century. The prime northeast corner of Fifth Avenue and 50th Street, where St. Patrick's Cathedral now stands opposite Rockefeller Center, was surrounded by undeveloped space for years after St. Patrick's was completed in 1878.

The turning point was the construction of Grand Central Terminal (1903–13). The project created not only a magnificent building, but also an elegant new boulevard covering the noisy, dirty, and dangerous expanse of open railroad tracks that had extended for blocks north of East 42nd Street. The new street, Park Avenue, was soon lined with office buildings and elegant hotels. One of the most famous, the Waldorf-Astoria, moved up in 1931 from its former home at 34th Street and Fifth Avenue, the current site of the Empire State Building. At its new address, it became the favorite hotel of U.S. presidents and other distinguished guests, such as the Duke of Windsor, Douglas MacArthur, Cole Porter, and Prince Rainier and Princess Grace of Monaco.

Once too far uptown to be fashionable, Fifth Avenue from East 50th to East 59th Street became the most elegant shopping street in the nation, with Tiffany's as the jewel in its crown. Farther east and later in the twentieth century, Bloomingdale's became Manhattan's trendiest department store for shoppers with disposable income. Across the street, a luxurious residential tower, One Beacon Court, is opening in 2005 as a vertical millionaire's row.

▶ **Grand Central Station:** *Elevated on a platform with a triumphal arched façade, the station is truly a grand gateway to the city. It opened in 1913 as the crowning glory of Cornelius Vanderbilt's New York Central Railroad. Half a century later, it was threatened with demolition, and became the* cause célèbre *of a successful historic preservation campaign, which was led by Jacqueline Kennedy Onassis.*

GRAND CENTRAL
TERMINAL

◄ **Grand Central Station Interior:** *The immense vaulted space inside the station has been called "the finest big room in the nation." Sunlight entering through the 75-foot-high windows casts long rays across the marble floor. The blue ceiling displays the constellations—from an unusual perspective. Seen from below, they are reversed, allowing the public "to see them as God would from the heavens above."*

▶ **Met Life Building:** *Once called a "monstrous wet blanket" because it cut off views of Park Avenue, the massive tower built behind Grand Central Terminal in 1963 has nonetheless become a fixture of this well-known scene. The spacious, multi-level lobby space, which leads into the terminal, is worth a visit.*

◀ **Chrysler Building:**
The pointed dome—the
culmination of the building's
imaginative Art Deco style—
once housed a lavish, three-
level "Cloud Club" for Chrysler
automobile executives. The
triangular windows recall the
spokes of a glittering hubcap,
or could be just part of the
fanciful design. Criticized as
ostentatious when it was built
in 1930, the Chrysler Building
is popular today—precisely
because of its flashy yet
sophisticated style.

▲ **Chrysler Building at
Night:** Lit from within its
triangular windows, the
Chrysler Building's lancet
dome is an ethereal presence
in the night sky. The lighting,
which formed part of the
original 1930 plans but was
not installed until 1981, has
become a unique feature of
the New York skyline.

Ford Foundation Building: *In the 1960s era of windowless offices locked into air-conditioned isolation, the Ford Foundation Building was a breath of fresh air. The twelve-story building has a ten-story skylit atrium lushly filled with full-growth trees and thousands of shrubs, vines, and plants. The offices overlook the garden court.*

◀ **Trump World Tower:**
The tallest residential building in the world when it was completed in 2001, this enormous tower caused an outcry from those who felt it was an overwhelming presence near the landmark United Nations. The loudest protests came from the residents of neighboring buildings, whose views were spoiled by this new big kid on the block. Although city officials tried to impose height limits for later buildings, the measure never gained widespread support.

▲ **United Nations Headquarters:** The most prominent building in the United Nations complex, the Secretariat tower (1953) was New York City's first glass-curtain wall. This type of construction, which hangs windows like a curtain on the steel frame, changed the face of modern architecture. The glass tower dramatically contrasts with the concrete, horizontal General Assembly Building around its base.

Citicorp Center: *By the time the Citicorp Building was completed in 1977, New Yorkers were no longer impressed by building height alone. At 900 feet, Citicorp was the third tallest in Midtown, but its distinctive sloped roof was the feature that made it a new star on the skyline. The round building to its lower right is known as the "Lipstick Building" for its round shape and pink hue.*

▶ **Seagram Building:**
This is the only New York City building by the acclaimed Modernist architect Ludwig Mies van der Rohe. It might not have happened at all, if not for the intervention of the daughter of Seagram's owner, who convinced her father to drop a mediocre design and hire the master architect in the early 1950s. The result was a new building that critics believe is a masterpiece of Modern design.

◀ **Lever House:** *Placed at right angles to the street, Lever House "floats" above Park Avenue. The gleaming glass box, which broke the mold of street design when it was built in 1952, stands apart in pristine isolation from its masonry neighbors.*

◀ **St. Bartholomew's Church (Café):** *Surrounded by terraces and open space, St. Bartholomew's, a Byzantine-style church, enjoys a rare luxury in New York City, standing alone on a crowded avenue. Its spacious grounds provide room for a popular outdoor café in the midst of Park Avenue.*

▶ **St. Patrick's Cathedral:** *Facing the statue of Atlas at Rockefeller Center, St. Patrick's occupies one of the most famous spots on Fifth Avenue. When it began construction in the mid-nineteenth century, paid for largely by the pennies of thousands of poor Irish-Americans, the cathedral rose on a relatively inexpensive plot. Today, the cathedral and its real estate are priceless.*

◀ **Waldorf-Astoria Hotel:** *Originally two separate hotels, the Waldorf and the Astoria were built in the 1890s by feuding cousins of the Astor family at another Manhattan location. The adjacent buildings functioned as a unit but could be sealed off at the ground level. Later generations mended fences and in 1931 built the existing Waldorf-Astoria, a massive Art Deco hotel on Park Avenue with more than 1400 rooms. The hotel restaurant, Oscar's, is famous for creating the Waldorf Salad, Veal Oscar, and Thousand Island dressing.*

▲ **One Beacon Court:**

Rising from an elliptical courtyard, this tower is the city's largest and most luxurious residential/office building. Designed by Cesar Pelli, it opened in 2005 with 105 condominiums, each one with a multi-million-dollar price tag. Lit at night, the crystalline tower is a new addition to the city skyline.

▶ **Four Seasons Hotel:**

I.M. Pei, the noted architect of this hotel, designs on a grand scale. His other major work in New York City is the vast Jacob Javits Convention Center (see page 72). Located on 57th Street, one of the busiest Midtown thoroughfares, the luxurious hotel lobby offers an awesome sense of space.

Central Park

Larger than most New York neighborhoods, Central Park makes a tremendous impact on the nation's most densely built urban environment. This green expanse of 843 acres—six percent of Manhattan's land area—provides immeasurable value to a narrow island packed with residents and visitors. Twenty-five million people come to the park each year to enjoy its zoos, lakes, playgrounds, restaurants, skating rinks, and 58 miles of pedestrian paths. Designed as a "pleasure ground" by America's greatest landscape visionary, Frederick Law Olmsted, it also has become the world's largest natural garden, with thousands of species of trees, plants, birds, mammals, and insects that have made their home in these man-made surroundings.

Building the park was an amazing undertaking—one of the largest public works projects of the nineteenth century. It took more than 20 years, from 1856 to 1878, interrupted, but not derailed, by the Civil War. During this time, 20,000 workers blasted out rock with more gunpowder than was used at the Battle of Gettysburg. They removed nearly three million cubic yards of soil, planted more than 270,000 trees and shrubs, and built a new reservoir within the park.

Today, amidst fierce competition for Manhattan real estate, the park demonstrates an incredible commitment to civic ideals by city leaders who set aside this much land in a growing metropolis for the future enjoyment of its citizens. It demonstrates, too, their brilliant foresight in increasing the value of the surrounding land. The park stimulated the development of the city's wealthiest neighborhoods. As they grew up around the park, the dramatic contrast of urban towers next to this green swath has made it all the more scenic and appealing.

▶ **Central Park Aerial:** *This dramatic view makes it quite clear that Central Park is the green heart of Manhattan. It is also the city's lungs, filtering the air through thousands of trees. And it is the city's playground, offering unlimited opportunities for the essential activities of urban life—recreation and relaxation.*

◀ **Bethesda Fountain:**

One of the most beautiful and popular spots in Central Park, the fountain was built to commemorate the city's clean water supply system established in the mid-nineteenth century. The figure at its top, "Angel of the Waters," was the inspiration for the contemporary play, Angels in America, *by New York playwright Tony Kushner.*

▲ **Central Park Lake:**

The park lake covers 20 acres, but seems much larger because of its many twists and turns. Created out of a swamp, it opened to the public years before the park was finished so that New Yorkers could have a place to enjoy two of the most popular recreational activities of the mid-nineteenth century, ice skating and boating. You can still rent a rowboat, or even take a gondola ride, just as New Yorkers did more than a century ago.

◄ **Central Park Wildlife
Center:** *Although most
people still call it the zoo, the
Wildlife Center is quite
different from the old zoo
model of small cages and
concrete floors. Ever since the
Wildlife Conservation Society
started managing the zoo in
1984, the emphasis has
changed to more natural
habitats. The sea-lion pool
shown here is equipped with
glass sides so that visitors
can see the sleek mammals
gliding through their spacious
underwater surroundings.*

▶ **Wollman Rink:** *The
New York craze for ice-
skating began during the
hard winter of 1858, when
Central Park's frozen lake
was first opened to the
public. Since winters were not
always cold enough to freeze
the lake, the Wollman Rink
was built in 1950 near the
59th Street entrance to the
park. It became an instant
success, drawing thousands of
people each day.*

▲ **Central Park Bow Bridge:** *Of the three dozen picturesque bridges in Central Park—each one a unique design—the Bow Bridge is the most revered. This graceful arch spans one of the lake's narrow turns. Although it looks like stone, it is, in fact, made of cast iron and built on an unusual and unseen foundation—cannon balls, which were used as moveable bearings to allow the cast iron to expand and contract.*

▶ **Plaza Hotel:** *Seen from the pond in Central Park and framed by more modern buildings, the historic Plaza Hotel owes much of its fame to its scenic location next to the park. Its Old World elegance was surprisingly appealing to the most original and non-traditional architect of the twentieth century, Frank Lloyd Wright: when in New York, he always stayed at the Plaza. The building began redevelopment in 2005 as a residential, retail, and hotel complex.*

Upper West Side

Striped down its length with grand boulevards and distinguished apartment buildings, the Upper West Side is a residential neighborhood with architectural character. Sandwiched between two major parks, it also enjoys precious proximity to green open space. From east to west, the neighborhood extends from Central Park to Riverside Park, which overlooks the Hudson River. From south to north, it reaches from 59th to 125th streets. Broadway, the commercial spine, tingles with bustling shops, restaurants, and movie houses.

Populated throughout its history with writers and people in the arts, the Upper West Side always had a cultural bent. Edgar Alan Poe wrote *The Raven* here in 1844 and Igor Stravinsky, Arturo Toscanini, Enrico Caruso, and many other legends of the musical world lived and worked in the Ansonia Hotel on Broadway. Opera, ballet, and classical music come together at Lincoln Center, the nexus of Manhattan's performing arts. Many popular celebrities were also Upper West Siders, including Babe Ruth, Humphrey Bogart, and former Beatle John Lennon, who lived and died here outside his home at the Dakota Apartments. Built for wealthy New Yorkers a century ago, many of the residential buildings went downhill after World War II, but regained their economic footing and cachet in later years.

Although it has become an expensive place to live once again, the neighborhood still retains its ethnic flavor: Zabar's, a gourmet emporium famous throughout the city, is one of many delicatessens offering food from every nation. The area also has a penchant for political activism. In the 1960s and '70s, Upper West Siders led scores of demonstrations against the Vietnam War and for civil rights and nuclear disarmament. During the 2004 presidential election campaign, the anti-Bush film, *Fahrenheit 9/11*, was sold out for weeks in the local movie theater.

▶ **Globe and Trump Hotel:** *Although Manhattan prides itself on setting the fashion for the other New York boroughs, the model for this globe comes from a much larger sphere in Queens. Donald Trump, who erected the globe and the luxury hotel behind it, also hails from Queens.*

◄ **Lincoln Center for the Performing Arts:** *This group of theaters for opera, ballet, and classical concerts has become a cultural landmark for the entire city. Built in the 1960s, the architectural style of the buildings is still a matter of debate, but the center, clustered around a large fountain and plaza, is an undisputed attraction and popular gathering place.*

▲ **Time Warner Center:** *A city within a building, this complex opened in 2003 with upscale shops and restaurants, three jazz performance centers, a luxury hotel, and high-rise apartments overlooking Central Park. It replaced the Coliseum, a building with a grand name but a boring design. The new center, designed by David Childs of Skidmore, Owings and Merrill, has a curved base that embraces Columbus Circle at the West 59th Street entrance to the park.*

American Museum of Natural History: *One of the city's largest and most popular museums, the Natural History Museum takes up four blocks and contains all types of beasts, large and small. Dinosaurs are among the biggest attractions. This space just inside the main entrance is dedicated to former President Theodore Roosevelt, an avid naturalist who led expeditions for the museum.*

Dakota Apartments: *When this château-esque building went up in 1884 as the city's first luxury apartment house, it was so far from other fashionable areas that New Yorkers compared it to living in the Dakotas. Today, it is the Upper West Side's most prestigious address. But it also has a darker side: John Lennon was murdered here in 1980 and it was also the setting for the Gothic movie thriller, Rosemary's Baby.*

Soldiers and Sailors Monument: *This massive temple-like structure in Riverside Park commemorates Union servicemen who fought in the Civil War. The design is based on the Choragic Monument of Lysicrates in Athens. Dedicated on Memorial Day, 1902, it was for years the terminus of New York City's annual Memorial Day parade.*

▲ **Riverside Park South Pier:** *Nearly 800 feet long, this pier can take you into the Hudson River, out with the seabirds and passing ships. It offers wonderful river views, a unique perspective of the city skyline, and a great place to fish. The pier once connected rail cars to floating barges. With its new scalloped edge, pastel paving, and high-tech lampposts and seats, it now connects people to the river in comfort and style.*

▶ **Rose Center for Earth and Space:** *The city's planetarium, this six-story-high glass cube cradling a blue-lit sphere is a dramatically different addition to the traditional streetscape of Central Park West. Unveiled at the start of the new millennium, it offers an exciting virtual trip into the galaxies. Its creator, New York-based architect James Polshek, calls it a "cosmic cathedral."*

HAYDEN PLANETARIUM

Upper East Side

Soon after Central Park was completed in the 1870s, Fifth Avenue was extended along the park and became Manhattan's Gold Coast. When a member of the famous Astor family built a château there in 1893, everyone knew the neighborhood had truly arrived. Steel-industry giants Henry Clay Frick and Andrew Carnegie, meatpacking magnate Herman Armour, and those of more delicate professions, such as art-glass designer Louis Comfort Tiffany, also built palatial homes on or just off the avenue. Known as the Silk Stocking District, the Upper East Side, from East 59th to 96th streets, remains one of the nation's wealthiest neighborhoods.

After World War I, many of the mansions were replaced by luxury apartment houses. But a number of the grand old houses survive today as splendid art museums on a stretch of Fifth Avenue known as Museum Mile. Its undisputed queen is the Metropolitan Museum of Art, a Versailles-like palace on the edge of Central Park.

The area east of the Gold Coast was lined with the modest homes of German and Irish immigrants. It began to change when the city built the East River Drive, constructed during World War II with rubble from buildings bombed during the London blitz. Cargo ships returning to New York from England carried the broken masonry in their holds as ballast. The Third Avenue elevated train tracks once overshadowed the eastern section, but after the el was torn down in the late 1950s, the area welcomed newfound light and air—and high-rise development. Since then, troops of luxury apartment towers have marched up the eastern side of the neighborhood, stretching the Silk Stocking District to the East River.

▶ **Upper East Side Homes:** *Upper East Side townhouses have a distinctive profile. Built for affluent families in the late nineteenth century, they still convey an aura of wealth and taste. The area is also known for its upscale Madison Avenue shopping district, several blocks of elite boutique stores.*

▲ **Frick Collection:** *After Henry Clay Frick and Andrew Carnegie ended their steel partnership in an acrimonious split, both of these multi-millionaires built mansions on Upper Fifth Avenue. Frick built a Beaux-Arts palace in 1914 that was designed to "make Carnegie's place look like a miner's shack." Frick's home, covering an entire block, is now a museum displaying his life-long art collection of European masterpieces.*

▶ **Roosevelt Island Tramway:** *An exhilarating aerial crossing, the tram was once just a daily commute for the residents of Roosevelt Island, a residential community developed in the 1970s across the East River from the Upper East Side. When a subway station opened on the island in 1989, the tram became a special event for tourists and commuters alike.*

◀ **Cooper-Hewitt National Museum of Design:** *Although Andrew Carnegie's 1901 mansion houses this museum, he was not involved in creating the institution. The Hewitts, granddaughters of another industrial giant, Peter Cooper, established the museum in 1896. It finally moved to the mansion in 1976. Every aspect of design is now on display—furniture, ceramics, glass, jewelry, textiles, rare books, drawings, and prints.*

▲ **Metropolitan Museum of Art:** *The most comprehensive art museum in the western hemisphere, the Met attracts millions of visitors each year to its palatial building on the edge of Central Park. Its Egyptian collection is second only to the one in Cairo. The striking setting within a modern glass wing of the Temple of Dendur—a gift from Egypt to the United States in 1965— makes this one of the Met's most dramatic exhibits.*

▲ **Guggenheim Museum, Exterior:** *The only major work by Frank Lloyd Wright in New York City, this spiral-shaped museum is the architect's best-known building. The unusual design made it the most controversial building ever to rise in the city when it opened in 1959. Since then it has become more acclaimed than its collection of modern art.*

▶ **Guggenheim Museum, Interior:** *Rising 75 feet from the gallery floor to the skylight, the museum interior is one large room displaying paintings along a spiraling ramp. Frank Lloyd Wright believed that following a continuous circular path was a great improvement over walking in and out of galleries in traditional museums. Critics still debate whether or not the unusual design detracts from the paintings.*

Museum of the City of New York: *Delving into the museum's treasury of books and artifacts from the city's history is an enjoyable way to find out what makes New York New York. The museum is known for its comprehensive collection of photographs, Currier and Ives prints, and theatrical materials documenting the golden age of Broadway.*

Northern Manhattan

Everyone has heard of Harlem, but not nearly as many know about the other neighborhoods in Manhattan's hilly northern terrain. Starting at the top, the Inwood neighborhood includes nearly 200 acres of primeval forest, the last one still standing in Manhattan. Once home to Native American cave dwellers, the steeply inclined forest is protected within Inwood Hill Park. Nearby is Dyckman House, the last surviving Dutch farmhouse in Manhattan, preserved as a museum.

Washington Heights, filled to its narrow borders with apartment houses and a maze of ethnic communities, was a choice location for country estates in colonial times because of the wonderful views overlooking the Hudson River. The Cloisters, a museum of medieval art housed in reconstructed French monasteries, now affords the same view to the public. The neighborhood is also the site of the Audubon Ballroom, where Malcolm X was slain.

John James Audubon, the naturalist artist, owned a farm nearby and is buried in a cemetery a few blocks away.

Harlem is much more than the stereotype of a black ghetto. It has rows of stately churches and homes, such as those on "Sugar Hill," where residents Cab Calloway, Duke Ellington, Thurgood Marshall, W.E.B. DuBois, Langston Hughes, and others enjoyed the "sweet" life. It also has more familiar attractions—soul-food restaurants and the Apollo Theater on 125th Street, where legendary singers and musicians performed. Former President Bill Clinton has offices nearby in a new office and entertainment complex. Just south of Harlem is Morningside Heights, dominated by Columbia University's large campus and beautiful Neo-Classical libraries. Two magnificent churches, the Cathedral of St. John the Divine and Riverside Church, are also striking landmarks.

▶ **Cathedral of St. John the Divine:** *This massive French Gothic cathedral in Morningside Heights was a response by Manhattan's socially prominent Episcopalians to St. Patrick's, the grand Roman Catholic Cathedral built by the city's Irish community. Planned as the world's largest cathedral, St. John's remains unfinished more than a century after its start. Despite its somewhat competitive beginnings in 1892, it became known as a progressive congregation, serving people from all walks of life.*

◄ **Riverside Church:**

Although it was modeled on Chartres Cathedral in France, this church on the southern edge of Harlem is a skyscraper at heart. Built on a steel frame, it rises 24 stories on a bluff above the Hudson River. Martin Luther King, Jr., delivered his famous anti-Vietnam War sermon from the pulpit, and Nelson Mandela also spoke here on his first visit to America.

▼ **Sylvan Terrace:**

Wooden rowhouses on a cobblestone street are a rare sight anywhere in New York City. This row from the 1880s, looking more like New Orleans than New York, is part of a charming historic district at Harlem's northern edge.

▷ **Harlem Brownstone:**

Rows of handsome brownstone homes line many Harlem streets. Named by Dutch colonial settlers, Harlem began as a remote farming village and became an urban neighborhood in the late nineteenth century. African-Americans began to live here in the early 1900s, seeking better housing and less racism than they encountered in other parts of the city. Within a few decades, the neighborhood became the nation's center of black economic, political, and cultural life.

◁ **George Washington Bridge:** *A startling design in its day, this bridge over the Hudson River to New Jersey was the first one built without any ornament. Completed in 1931, it was all bare steel without any cladding or architectural flourishes on its towers. Modernist architect Le Corbusier described it as "the most beautiful bridge in the world."*

△ **Morris-Jumel Mansion:** *One of the few surviving buildings in Manhattan pre- dating the Revolutionary War, the mansion was built in 1765 by British Colonel Roger Morris. George Washington claimed it as his headquarters during the Battle of Harlem Heights in the first year of the war. French emigrant Stephen Jumel and his wife Eliza made it their stylish home in 1811. After Jumel's death, Eliza married notorious Aaron Burr who had killed Alexander Hamilton in a duel in 1804. She soon divorced him and fought a long court battle to keep the mansion. Some say her ghost still haunts the house.*

▲ **The Cloisters:** *Sections of five medieval monasteries from France were reassembled in this hilltop setting in Fort Tryon Park to recreate an ensemble of enchanting rooms, passageways, and gardens. In all, the museum houses 5000 works of art from medieval Europe, including stained-glass windows and the famous Unicorn Tapestries.*

▶ **Little Red Lighthouse, Washington Heights:** *This tiny structure under the Manhattan tower of the George Washington Bridge owes its survival to a 1942 children's story,* The Little Red Lighthouse and the Great Gray Bridge. *In the story, the lighthouse "worries" that the bridge's towering lights will make it obsolete. In fact, the lighthouse was put on the auction block in 1951. After an outpouring of support from children and parents throughout the country, the lighthouse was declared a national landmark in 1979.*

Index

Manhattan Map

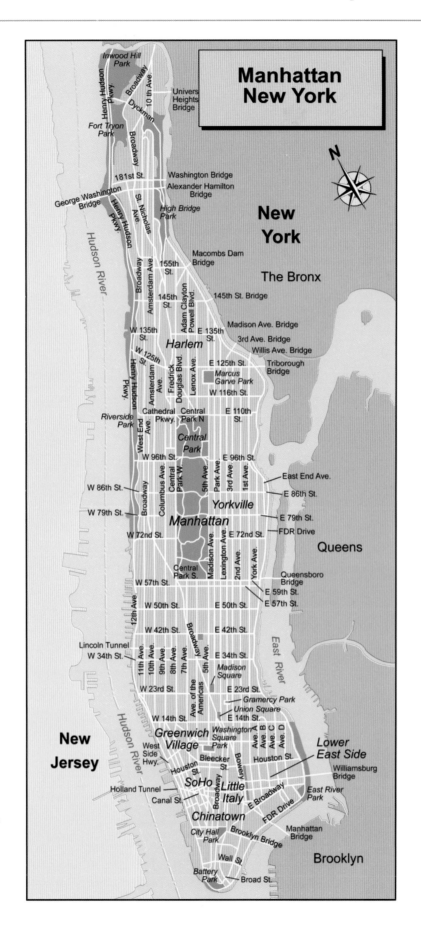